The 30 Day Writing Workout for Fiction Authors

12 Minutes A Day
Writing for the Non-Writer

The Blogging Edition 1

By Renee Settle

DEDICATION

For those of us who are just starting and want to DIY with purpose.

Thank you for the lessons I learned while writing this workbook..

Your story matters. My story matters. Together, our stories will change the world.

12 MINUTES A DAY FOR FICTION AUTHORSS
INSTRUCTIONS

An introduction to the 12 Minutes A Day method for fiction authors, the blogging edition #1!

I've used the 12 Minutes A Day method for many different exercises. Some 12MAD methods include questions to answer. I've honed this method to include some drawing. Not because I think writers can draw, because I sure cannot. But because it engages my brain in a different way and awakens my creative muse faster. She probably feels the pressure of the competition, I'm not sure. In any case, it works and that's all that matters. We authors can spend all day, every day creating worlds and making amazing prose, but when it comes to communicating with our readers, we freeze up faster than SubZero's freeze ray gun or whatever fictional equivalent suits your genre. SO, here are the rules, loosely applied, of course!

Tools you will need:
- A pencil, a pen, crayons, or colored pens or pencils. Whatever you feel most comfortable with using. You can even use a computer. The key is to make sure you are comfortable. I recommend hand writing it the first time because it will help you slow down and think. Sometimes our lives get so urgent that we don't take time to think. This process will help you take just twelve minutes to focus on one thing and complete it successfully.
- A way to time yourself. You will use something that will alert you at the end of two (2) minutes and ten (10) minutes. A smart phone usually works well for this. However, I've known people who use an egg timer shaped like a rooster. Whatever makes it fun and relaxing for you is important.
- Bring your imagination, well, the truth is, you can't go anywhere without it, so you should be used to it by now..

That's IT! Just those three things.

NOW, here are the steps. Each day, you will practice these steps. So don't worry about getting it right the first time.

Practice Makes Perfect!

1. Open the book to the prompt you'll be working on.
2. Read the prompt carefully and make sure you understand it.
3. Set the timer for two (2) minutes.
4. Start the timer and draw a picture representation of what the prompt makes you think of. It doesn't have to be perfect or even understandable to anyone else. The key point here is to draw something you can relate to the topic. We are giving your brain time to process the prompt.
5. When the timer alerts, evaluate your drawing. Is it complete to your satisfaction? If it's not, reset the timer repeat step four (4). Do not stop drawing until the timer alerts you. Even if you trace over the same drawing, don't stop until it rings.
6. Now, review your drawing and reset your timer for ten (10) minutes.
7. Start the timer and write the blog that goes with the prompt. Whatever you do, don't stop writing. If you get distracted, write the thoughts in your head. Keep writing until the alarm rings.
8. If you haven't finished your thoughts, reset the timer and repeat step seven (7) until you feel comfortable. You may use other paper if there isn't enough room in the workbook. .

Remember, this is a minimum, if you aren't done after twelve (12) minutes, set the timer for another twelve (12)) minutes and keep writing.

CONGRATULATIONS!

YOU'VE WRITTEN FOR 12 MINUTES!

PLEASE NOTE:

1. This exercise isn't about good grammar, sentence structure or spelling. It's about writing down the idea, first. You can always go back later and edit it.
2. These steps are flexible. If you already know what you want to write and you think it's not necessary for you to draw anything, then set your timer for twelve (12) minutes and go to town! The idea is to write a blog. This tool set is designed to help you break free of a block. That means if you don't have a block and you just needed the prompt, then, this method has still worked!
JUST WRITE IT!

Once you're done with the workout, you can go back to each blog and edit, r
efine, add to, or take away from what you've written. You can even send it out to be edited. I'll be happy to help you with that. My contact information is on the last page.

Now you're ready to write your blogs!

NUMBER 1

Why did you decide to start writing fiction? Write as if you're telling your best friend.

DRAW IT BELOW

WRITE THE BLOG

NUMBER 2

What is your favorite tool, either online or offline, to use for when you write?

DRAW IT BELOW

WRITE THE BLOG

_____

_____

_____

_____

_____

_____

_____

_____

_____

_____

_____

_____

_____

_____

_____

_____

NUMBER 3

If there was one talent you wished you had, what would it be and why?

DRAW IT BELOW

WRITE THE BLOG

NUMBER 4

What's your favorite holiday? Why? What do you like most about it? How does it make you feel?

DRAW IT BELOW

WRITE THE BLOG

_____

_____

_____

_____

_____

_____

_____

_____

_____

_____

_____

_____

_____

_____

_____

_____

NUMBER 5

Who is your favorite character you've written about?
Why are they your favorite?

DRAW IT BELOW

WRITE THE BLOG

_____

_____

_____

_____

_____

_____

_____

_____

_____

_____

_____

_____

_____

_____

_____

_____

NUMBER 6

What is your favorite quote from a story you've written? Write the quote and why you love it so much.

DRAW IT BELOW

WRITE THE BLOG

_____

_____

_____

_____

_____

_____

_____

_____

_____

_____

_____

_____

_____

_____

_____

_____

NUMBER 7

Define an overall problem a main character has experienced in your book(s). Why does this affect them so?

DRAW IT BELOW

WRITE THE BLOG

_____

_____

_____

_____

_____

_____

_____

_____

_____

_____

_____

_____

_____

_____

_____

_____

You have written for seven days!

Celebrate!

DON'T STOP NOW!
Keep going!

12 Minutes A Day
Writing for the Non-Writer

NUMBER 8

It's Easter. How would a character in your story celebrate it? What is important to them about this holiday?

DRAW IT BELOW

WRITE THE BLOG

NUMBER 9

What if your character visited a museum? Write about something they discovered and how it affected them.

DRAW IT BELOW

WRITE THE BLOG

_____

_____

_____

_____

_____

_____

_____

_____

_____

_____

_____

_____

_____

_____

_____

_____

_____

NUMBER 10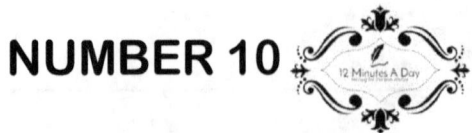

Think of something you could give away. Write about it and why you decided on that particular giveaway.

DRAW IT BELOW

WRITE THE BLOG

NUMBER 11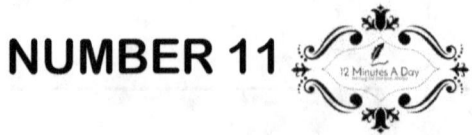

Who is your favorite movie star? Why? What movies would you recommend your clients see that star this person?

DRAW IT BELOW

WRITE THE BLOG

_____

_____

_____

_____

_____

_____

_____

_____

_____

_____

_____

_____

_____

_____

_____

NUMBER 12

Write a thank you to your favorite reader (make one up if you don't have one. Give them a name and everything!). Explain in detail why they are being showcased and what you love about them.

DRAW IT BELOW

WRITE THE BLOG

_____

_____

_____

_____

_____

_____

_____

_____

_____

_____

_____

_____

_____

_____

_____

_____

NUMBER 13

Do you have a new story? Highlight the details and write about the reason you developed this story. What will the reader experience?

DRAW IT BELOW

WRITE THE BLOG

CONGRATULATIONS!
You have written for fourteen days!

NOW call yourself a blogger!

You are halfway there!

NUMBER 14

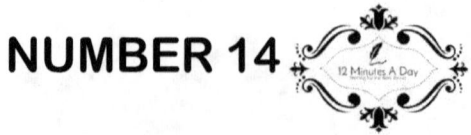

Do you think that new technology is always a good thing? Write about an example where it has done more harm than good.

DRAW IT BELOW

WRITE THE BLOG

NUMBER 15

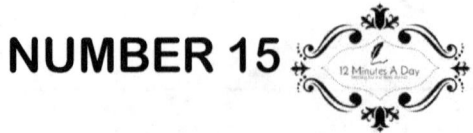

Make a list of things you wish you'd known when you first started writing. Then explain why these would be helpful for someone else starting out.

DRAW IT BELOW

WRITE THE BLOG

NUMBER 16

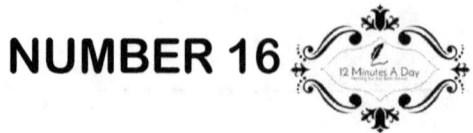

What is your favorite business book? Explain how it's helped you and why your readers or other writiers should read it.

DRAW IT BELOW

WRITE THE BLOG

_____

_____

_____

_____

_____

_____

_____

_____

_____

_____

_____

_____

_____

_____

_____

NUMBER 17

Write down questions you want to ask your customers about their experience. Tell them why you want the answers and how it will help your business.

DRAW IT BELOW

WRITE THE BLOG

NUMBER 18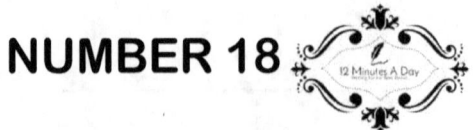

It's Veterans Day.   Write a post about what that means to a character you've written about.   Be specific as possible. Write it as an interview.

DRAW IT BELOW

WRITE THE BLOG

NUMBER 19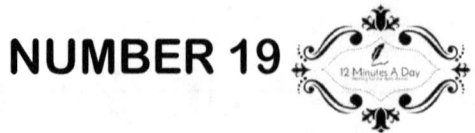

Today is reader appreciation day! Write a thank letter to all your readers (there are millions of them!). Detail exactly why they are so important to you and how they've helped you grow personally and professionally.

DRAW IT BELOW

WRITE THE BLOG

_____

_____

_____

_____

_____

_____

_____

_____

_____

_____

_____

_____

_____

_____

_____

_____

NUMBER 20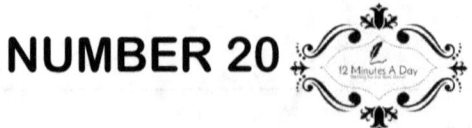

What do you think is the best invention of all time? Explain why you think so!

DRAW IT BELOW

WRITE THE BLOG

_____

_____

_____

_____

_____

_____

_____

_____

_____

_____

_____

_____

_____

_____

_____

_____

NUMBER 21

What is the strangest thing you have ever seen? What were you doing when you saw it? Tell the story as if you are telling your best friend about it!

DRAW IT BELOW

WRITE THE BLOG

_____

_____

_____

_____

_____

_____

_____

_____

_____

_____

_____

_____

_____

_____

_____

YOU ARE A ROCK STAR!

You've written twenty-one blogs!

Treat yourself to something nice!

You're almost there!
Keep writing!

NUMBER 22

What is your favorite vacation spot? Write a story about one of your characters visiting that spot. What would a typical day be like there for them?

DRAW IT BELOW

WRITE THE BLOG

_____

_____

_____

_____

_____

_____

_____

_____

_____

_____

_____

_____

_____

_____

_____

_____

NUMBER 23

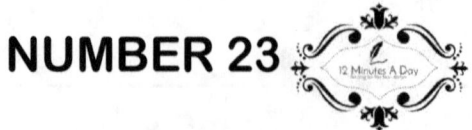

Do you have a writer that inspires you? Write about that person and why they are so inspirational.

DRAW IT BELOW

WRITE THE BLOG

_____

_____

_____

_____

_____

_____

_____

_____

_____

_____

_____

_____

_____

_____

_____

_____

NUMBER 24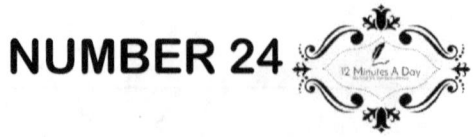

"I write to give myself strength. I write to be the characters that I am not. I write to explore all the things I'm afraid of." -- Joss Whedan. Describe what that phrase means to you. Do you have a life example of this? What happened?

DRAW IT BELOW

WRITE THE BLOG

_____

_____

_____

_____

_____

_____

_____

_____

_____

_____

_____

_____

_____

_____

_____

_____

NUMBER 25

Is there something most people don't know about you? Write about it in detail.

DRAW IT BELOW

WRITE THE BLOG

_____

_____

_____

_____

_____

_____

_____

_____

_____

_____

_____

_____

_____

_____

_____

_____

_____

NUMBER 26

When you were growing up, did you have a favorite television show? What was most memorable about it? Why would you recommend someone watch it today?

DRAW IT BELOW

WRITE THE BLOG

NUMBER 27

Did you ever have a memorable customer service experience? Write about it. What do you think made it the most memorable? How did you apply that knowledge to your writing?

DRAW IT BELOW

WRITE THE BLOG

_____

_____

_____

_____

_____

_____

_____

_____

_____

_____

_____

_____

_____

_____

_____

_____

NUMBER 28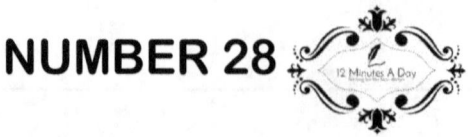

Write a story about the day you forgot something very important. What did you forget? What happened? How did you decide to remember next time?

DRAW IT BELOW

WRITE THE BLOG

NUMBER 29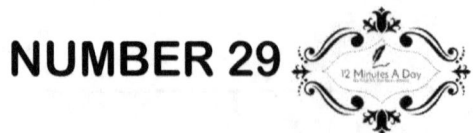

Do you have an easy life hack? Write about it. Use step by step instructions.

DRAW IT BELOW

WRITE THE BLOG

_____

_____

_____

_____

_____

_____

_____

_____

_____

_____

_____

_____

_____

_____

_____

_____

NUMBER 30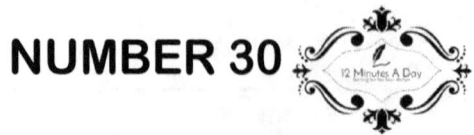

How has your genre grown since you started? Write about the pros and the cons and give your personal opinion on each of them.

DRAW IT BELOW

WRITE THE BLOG

_____

_____

_____

_____

_____

_____

_____

_____

_____

_____

_____

_____

_____

_____

_____

_____

YOU ARE AN AUTHOR BLOGGER!
YOU have finished the 30 Day Writing Workout for FICTION AUTHORS! Now you have 30 days of blog posts!

12 Minutes A Day
Writing for the Non-Writer

ABOUT THE AUTHOR

Renee Settle – Renee is a master coach, published author, and writer/editor consultant for hire. She is the inventor of 12 Minutes A Day, Writing for the Non-Writer. She is passionate about peoples stories and believes everyone has a story to write. She developed 12 Minutes A Day to help people do just that. Write their stories. Her motto is "Your Story Matters. My Story Matters. Together, our stories will change the world!" You can find her hanging out on her website at www.12minutestory.com. Or at www.reneesettle.com

She can be found on social media:
Email: renee@reneesettle.com
Facebook (facebook.com/12minutestory)
Twitter (@12minutestory)
Instagram (@12minutestory).